Informing the legislative debate since 1914 _____

Mongolia: Issues for Congress

Susan V. Lawrence
Specialist in Asian Affairs

June 17, 2014

Congressional Research Service

7-5700

www.crs.gov

R41867

Summary

Mongolia is a sparsely populated young democracy in a remote part of Asia, sandwiched between two powerful large neighbors, China and Russia. It made its transition to democracy and free market reforms peacefully in 1990, after nearly 70 years as a Soviet satellite state. A quarter of a century later, the predominantly Tibetan Buddhist nation remains the only formerly Communist Asian nation to have embraced democracy. Congress has shown a strong interest in Mongolia since 1990, funding assistance programs, approving the transfer of excess defense articles, ratifying a bilateral investment treaty, passing legislation to extend permanent normal trade relations, and passing seven resolutions commending Mongolia's progress and supporting strong U.S.-Mongolia relations.

Congressional interest is Mongolia has focused on the country's story of democratic development. Since passing a democratic constitution in 1992, Mongolia has held six direct presidential elections and six direct parliamentary elections. The State Department considers Mongolia's most recent elections to have been generally "free and fair" and said that in 2013, Mongolia "generally respected" freedoms of speech, press, assembly, and association. It raised concerns, however, about corruption and lack of transparency in government affairs.

On the economic front, Mongolia's mineral wealth, including significant reserves of coal, copper, gold, and uranium, offers investment opportunities for American companies. Foreign investors and the U.S. government have criticized Mongolia's unpredictable investment climate, however. In the fall of 2013, Mongolia passed a new investment law and, after years of negotiations, signed a transparency agreement with the United States. Both developments served to reassure investors, although the Mongolian parliament has yet to ratify the transparency agreement.

Mongolia was among the first nations to join the coalition for the Iraq War and its troops have been deployed in Afghanistan since 2003. It is also an active contributor of troops to United Nations Peacekeeping Operations and, with the United States, hosts an annual multinational peacekeeping exercise in Mongolia known as Khaan Quest.

Mongolia is an active participant in many international organizations, in which it often supports U.S. positions. It has also been an active member of international groupings dedicated to promoting democracy, including the Community of Democracies, for which it held the rotating chairmanship from 2011 to 2013. In the summer of 2014, Mongolia is scheduled to take over the rotating chairmanship of the Freedom Online Coalition, which describes itself as "an inter-governmental coalition committed to advancing Internet freedom—free expression, association, assembly, and privacy online—worldwide." Mongolia is also in the process of joining the Open Government Partnership, a White House-backed multilateral initiative.

Mongolia seeks to maintain "balanced relations" with its two immediate neighbors, China and Russia. China has emerged as Mongolia's largest trading partner and foreign investor. Russia is Mongolia's largest source of energy products. Mongolia has diplomatic relations with both North and South Korea and has sought to play a role in reducing tensions on the Korean Peninsula. To ensure its continued independence and sovereignty, Mongolia has also prioritized the development of relations with so-called "third neighbors," countries that do not border Mongolia, but have close ties to Mongolia. That list includes the United States. In 1992, Mongolia declared itself a single-state nuclear-weapons-free zone; in 2012, the five permanent members of the UN Security Council each pledged to respect the designation.

Contents

Tables

Appendixes

Contacts

Overview

Mongolia is a vast, sparsely populated, mineral-rich nation sandwiched between Russia and China. Formerly a Soviet satellite state, the country peacefully ended one-party Communist rule and launched democratic and free market reforms in 1990. Congress has shown strong support for Mongolia since that date through funding of assistance programs, approval for the transfer of excess defense articles, ratification of a bilateral investment treaty, extension of permanent normal trade relations, and House, Senate, and concurrent resolutions commending Mongolia on its development of democracy and expressing support for expanded U.S.-Mongolia relations. (See **Appendix A** for a list of significant legislation related to Mongolia from the 102nd Congress to the present.) Mongolia's is one of 16 parliaments worldwide that have been partnered with the U.S. House Democracy Partnership, a bipartisan, 20-member commission of the U.S. House of Representatives that has worked to support the development of "effective, independent, and responsive legislative institutions."[2]

Mongolia: Basic Information[1]
Population (2012): 2.796 million
Nominal GDP (2012 est.): $10.27 billion
Per capita GDP (2012): $3,160
GDP growth rate (2013 est.): 12.5%
Projected GDP growth rates: 10.3% for 2014; 10% for 2015; 7.7% for 2016
Inflation (2013): 9.6%
Percent of population at or below national poverty line (2012): 27.4
Predominant religion: Tibetan Buddhist (55.1% of population)

U.S. interests in Mongolia include what a 2011 U.S.-Mongolia Joint Statement refers to as "common values and shared strategic interests." Most prominent is the two nations' "common interest in protecting and promoting freedom, democracy and human rights worldwide."[3] Mongolia is the only formerly Communist Asian nation to have transitioned to democracy, and regards itself as a potential role model for the nations of Central Asia, and even China and North Korea, as well as for nations in other regions of the world attempting democratic transitions. In a statement issued after Mongolian President Tsakhiagiin Elbegdorj's re-election in 2013, President Obama stated that, "Through its impressive democratic achievements and its progress on economic liberalization, Mongolia serves as a significant example of positive reform and transformation for peoples around the world."[4]

As Mongolia begins to approve deals for development of its so far largely untapped mineral wealth, estimated to be worth hundreds of billions of dollars, the United States has an interest in strengthening the investment climate for U.S. businesses in Mongolia. The United States also has an interest in many aspects of Mongolia's engagement with the broader international community. Mongolia has contributed troops to the wars in Iraq and Afghanistan, and to global United Nations Peacekeeping Operations. It has supported U.S. positions in international organizations such as the United Nations, and embraced international democracy promotion initiatives.

---

[1] Economic data is from The World Bank, "Data: Mongolia," http://data.worldbank.org/country/mongolia, accessed June 5, 2014; religion data is from The Pew Forum on Religion & Public Life, *The Global Religious Landscape: A Report on the Size and Distribution of the World's Major Religious Groups as of 2010*, December 2012, http://www.pewforum.org/files/2014/01/global-religion-full.pdf.

[2] For more information, see the website of the House Democracy Partnership: http://hdac.house.gov/.

[3] The White House, "U.S.-Mongolia Joint Statement," June 16, 2011, http://www.whitehouse.gov/the-press-office/2011/06/16/us-mongolia-joint-statement.

[4] The White House, "Statement by President on the Presidential Election in Mongolia," June 27, 2013, http://www.whitehouse.gov/the-press-office/2013/06/27/statement-president-presidential-election-mongolia.

Uranium-rich Mongolia also has taken a strong stance in support of nuclear non-proliferation. As a nation with diplomatic relations with both North and South Korea, Mongolia has sought to support peace and stability on the Korean Peninsula. With a majority Tibetan Buddhist population and close ties to Tibet's exiled spiritual leader, the Dalai Lama, Mongolia also has a strong interest in Tibet's future.

Democratic Development

For nearly 70 years, Mongolia was a one-party state ruled by the communist Mongolian People's Revolutionary Party (MPRP). Mongolia's democratic revolution began with Eastern Europe-inspired street protests in western Mongolia in December 1989, which then spread to the capital, Ulaanbaatar. The MPRP's Politburo chose to resign en masse in March 1990. Since then, Mongolia has made a rapid transition from one-party Communist rule to multi-party parliamentary democracy. In May 1990, constitutional amendments ended the MPRP's monopoly on power and created an indirectly-elected presidency. In 1992, a new democratic constitution guaranteed a broad set of rights and freedoms, created a directly-elected presidency, and established a multi-party, directly-elected, unicameral legislature, the State Great Hural (SGH).[5] Since then, Mongolia has held six direct presidential elections and six direct parliamentary elections. (See **Appendix B** for the results of all ten elections.)

Mongolia's revised "National Security Concept," passed by the Mongolian parliament in 2010, reaffirmed Mongolia's commitment to democracy, stating that, "Parliamentary governance built on respect for human rights and freedoms, the rule of law, as well as a democratic state structure built on social stability shall be the pre-eminent guarantee for the assurance of national security."[6] Congress has passed resolutions congratulating Mongolia on a series of largely free and fair elections, and the State Department said that in 2013, Mongolia "generally respected" freedoms of speech, press, assembly, and association.[7]

Challenges to Democracy and Human Rights

Mongolia's democratic development remains a work in progress. In its report on human rights practices in Mongolia in 2013, the State Department highlighted three serious human rights problems facing Mongolia: "police abuse of detainees, widespread corruption, and a lack of transparency in government affairs." According to the report, "Ample documentation establishes both that corruption was widespread and that the perception and reality of corruption were serious drags on democratic and economic development." Such issues are a concern to those who see a strong Mongolian democracy as vital to keeping Mongolia a neutral, sovereign country that is able to stand up for its interests in the face of its powerful neighbors, China and Russia. (For more information about Mongolia's efforts to increase government transparency, see "U.S.-Mongolia Transparency Agreement" and "Participation in International Democracy Promotion" below.)

---

[5] Also sometimes rendered as State Great Khural or the Mongolian Great Khural or Mongolian Great Hural.

[6] *National Security Concept of Mongolia,* July 15, 2010. English translation provided by the Embassy of Mongolia to the United States.

[7] U.S. Department of State, *2013 Country Reports on Human Rights Practices: Mongolia,* February 27, 2014, http://www.state.gov/j/drl/rls/hrrpt/humanrightsreport/index htm?year=2013&dlid=220215.

In a USAID-supported survey of the Mongolian business community in May 2013, 69.1% of respondents said that they "always" or "often" encountered corruption in public sector tenders and contracting, and 62.4% of respondents said they believed that steps taken by the government to control corruption were "hardly effective" or "not at all effective." The report warned that private sector corruption "makes Mongolia vulnerable to bad governance and chronic income inequality among citizens."[8] Transparency International's Corruption Perceptions Index for 2013 ranked Mongolia 83rd of 177 countries in the index, with the top ranked country (Denmark) being the least corrupt. Mongolia shared its ranking with seven other nations: Burkina Faso, El Salvador, Jamaica, Liberia, Peru, Trinidad and Tobago, and Zambia.[9] Other concerns raised in the State Department report include, "arbitrary arrests; poor conditions in detention centers; government interference with the media; religious discrimination (including continued refusal by some provincial governments to register Christian churches); denial of exit visas and immigration holds on foreign citizens; inadequate measures to counter domestic violence against women; trafficking in persons; discrimination against persons with disabilities; and violence and discrimination against lesbian, gay, bisexual, and transgender (LGBT) persons."[10]

The Corruption Case Against Former President Enkhbayar

In April 2012, Mongolia's Independent Authority Against Corruption (IAAC) arrested former President Nambaryn Enkhbayar and charged him with corruption and fraud.[11] Enkhbayar, who served as president from 2005 to 2009, as speaker of the parliament from 2004-2005, and as Prime Minister from 2000-2004, remains the most high-profile figure in Mongolia ever to be charged with corruption. His case ignited impassioned debate in Mongolia. Some saw it as an object lesson in the difficulty of holding a politically powerful and internationally-connected figure to account. Others saw it as a politically-driven vendetta that brought into question Mongolia's commitment to human rights and the rule of law.

Immediately after the former president's arrest, his supporters denounced the charges as politically motivated. His son, a United States-educated banker, described the government's treatment of his father as "a purge" and alleged that the government sought "to keep him away from the election and remove him from politics."[12] Enkhbayar was then, and remains today, head of the Mongolian People's Revolutionary Party (MPRP), a breakaway party formed in 2011after the original MPRP changed its name to the Mongolian People's Party. Enkhbayar's arrest came two months before parliamentary elections and it made him ineligible to run for office. Had Enkhbayar been able to stand and had he won a seat, he would have gained parliamentary immunity. The IAAC stated that it had sought to question Enkhbayar for months, and arrested him only after he repeatedly ignored its summonses.

---

[8] The Asia Foundation, *Study of Private Perceptions of Corruption,* September 2013, http://asiafoundation.org/publications/pdf/1199.

[9] Transparency International, *Corruption Perceptions Index 2013*, http://cpi.transparency.org/cpi2013/results/.

[10] U.S. Department of State, *2013 Country Reports on Human Rights Practices: Mongolia*, February 27, 2014, http://www.state.gov/j/drl/rls/hrrpt/humanrightsreport/index htm?year=2013&dlid=220215.

[11] The Independent Authority Against Corruption, Press Release, May 11, 2012, http://www.iaac mn/index.php?coid=1618&cid=17.

[12] Dan Levin, "Ex-Leader's Detention Tests Mongolia's Budding Democracy," *The New York Times*, May 13, 2012, http://www nytimes.com/2012/05/14/world/asia/mongolias-democracy-tested-by-ex-presidents-arrest html.

Enkhbayar was convicted at his first trial in August 2012 and sentenced to four years in prison. On appeal before the Supreme Court in December 2012, he was again convicted and this time sentenced to two-and-a-half years in prison. Throughout the process, his supporters alleged a variety of official abuses, from denial of adequate medical care, to denial of access to family and legal counsel, to judicial bias and procedural problems. Influential figures in the international community, including UN Secretary General Bank Ki-moon, expressed concern about the government's treatment of the former president. In its 2012 report on human rights practices in Mongolia, however, the State Department stated that, "Observers of the four postponement hearings and trials, which were televised and open to the public, generally found the process in compliance with law."[13]

With Enkhbayar reportedly in ill health, President Tsakhiagiin Elbegdorj issued a terse decree on August 1, 2013 pardoning him and ordering him released from the remainder of his sentence.[14] Canadian Mongolia expert Julian Dierkes explained the pardon as a move that "deflects accusations against Elbegdorj and the DP [Democratic Party] that they are partisan in their pursuit of anti-corruption measures and makes the president look more like a head of state above the political fray."[15] Enkhbayar subsequently traveled to South Korea for medical treatment, where he remains today. He has been reported to be planning a political comeback.[16]

Institutions and Electoral Procedures

Presidential elections are held every four years, with the next presidential election scheduled for 2017. Each political party represented in Mongolia's parliament is permitted to nominate one candidate, with the winner requiring a simple majority of the popular vote. The President serves as head of state, commander in chief of the armed forces, and head of the National Security Council. He can veto all or some of laws passed by parliament, although parliament may override his veto. He may serve no more than two terms of four years each. One of the quirks of the Mongolian system is that the President is required to give up his party affiliation upon taking office.

Elections to Mongolia's Parliament, the State Great Hural, are held every four years in June, with the next election scheduled for 2016. The State Great Hural has 76 members representing 26 multi-member constituencies. Once the State Great Hural is elected, members choose a speaker, the chairman of the State Great Hural, who ranks second in the state hierarchy and serves as an *ex officio* member of the National Security Council. The State Great Hural also nominates the prime minister and the cabinet, who are formally proposed to the State Great Hural by the president. The State Great Hural meets semi-annually for sessions of at least 75 days.[17]

---

[13] U.S. Department of State, 2012 Country Reports on Human Rights Practices: Mongolia, http://www.state.gov/j/drl/ rls/hrrpt/2012humanrightsreport/index htm#wrapper; James T. Areddy, "Mongolia Was Under Pressure Over Presidential Detention," *The Wall Street Journal* blogs, May 15, 2012, http://blogs.wsj.com/dispatch/2012/05/15/ mongolia-was-under-pressure-over-presidential-detention/.

[14] The Office of the President of Mongolia, Public Relations & Communications Division, "Decree of the President of Mongolia," August 1, 2013, http://www.president mn/eng/newsCenter/viewNews.php?newsId=934.

[15] Julian Dierkes, "Does Presidential Pardon Bring End to Enkhbayar Saga?" *Mongolia Focus* blog, August 15, 2013, http://blogs.ubc.ca/mongolia/2013/end-enkhbayar-saga/.

[16] "Enkhbayar Promises Political Comeback," January 6, 2014, News mn, http://english news.mn/content/166816.shtml

[17] *Parliament of Mongolia - State Great Hural*, webpage for the 19th annual meeting of the Asia Pacific Parliamentary Forum, Ulaanbaatar, Mongolia, 23-27 January 2011, text dated November 13, 2010, http://19appf.parliament.mn/ (continued...)

Election Outcomes

The formerly Communist MPRP, which changed its name to the Mongolian People's Party (MPP) in December 2010, won three of the presidential elections since 1992 and won the most seats in four of the parliamentary elections. Since 2012, the Democratic Party has controlled the positions of President, Prime Minister, and Chairman of the State Great Hural. In the most recent parliamentary election in June 2012, the Democratic Party won 33 of the 76 seats in the State Great Hural. It leads a coalition government including the Justice Coalition (comprised of a new MPRP party, formed in early 2011 by a faction that split from the re-named MPP, and the Mongolian National Democratic Party) and the Civil Will-Green Party. The MPP, with 25 seats, now serves as the opposition party. President Tsakhiagiin Elbegdorj, Mongolia's first president from the Democratic Party, was re-elected to a second four-year term in June 2013. (See text box, **Mongolia's Leaders**.)

Mongolia's Leaders[18]

President: Tsakhiagiin Elbegdorj of the Democratic Party (since May 2009)

Born in 1963, Elbegdorj is the first president of Mongolia from the Democratic Party. A former journalist, Elbegdorj was one of the original 13 leaders of the 1990 democratic revolution. He led the Democratic Union Coalition (DUC) to a historic victory over the formerly communist Mongolian People's Revolutionary Party in parliamentary elections in 1996. Elbegdorj served twice as Prime Minister, first for a brief period in 1998 and again from 2004-2006. Elbegdorj studied journalism at a military academy in the Soviet Union from 1983-1988, in the city of Lviv, which is now in western Ukraine. In 2002 he earned a Master's in Public Administration from the Kennedy School of Government at Harvard University. As a member of a small western Mongolian tribe, the Zahchin, he is the first president not to be a member of the dominant ethnic group in Mongolia, the Khalkha.[19] Elbegdorj won re-election in 2013. He is limited to two terms in office, which would end in 2017.

Prime Minister: Norovyn Altankhuyag of the Democratic Party (since August 2012)

Born in 1958, Altankhuyag has served as leader of the Democratic Party since 2008. He is a former teacher of biophysics and physics at the National University of Mongolia who played a prominent role in the 1990 democratic revolution. Before becoming Prime Minister, Altankhuyag served as Minister of Finance (2004-2006) and Minister of Agriculture and Industry (1996-2000), and was elected three times to Mongolia's parliament, the State Great Hural (1996, 2008, and 2012).[20]

Chairman of the State Great Hural: Zandaakhuu Enkhbold of the Democratic Party (since 2012)

Born in 1966, Enkhbold has been a member of parliament since 2004. He served as Chairman of the State Great Hural's Standing Committee on Security and Foreign Policy from 2008 to 2011. Originally trained as an electrical engineer, Enkhbold earned a law degree from the National University of Mongolia in 1996 and an MBA from the University of Denver in 2004. He served as Chairman of Mongolia's State Property Committee from 1996 to 1999, overseeing the country's privatization process.[21]

(...continued)

index.php?option=com_content&view=article&id=13:2010-11-13-06-10-11&catid=13:2010-11-13-04-15-34&Itemid=26.

[18] Biographical data from Alan J.K. Sanders, *Historical Dictionary of Mongolia*, 3rd ed. (The Scarecrow Press, Inc., 2010).

[19] Uradyn E. Bulag, "Mongolia in 2009: From Landlocked to Land-linked Cosmopolitan," vol. 50, no. 1 (2010), p. 98.

[20] "The 27th Prime Minister of Mongolia Norov Altankhuyag Starts His Office Term," InfoMongolia.com, August 10, 2012, http://www.infomongolia.com/ct/ci/4725.

[21] Official website of the State Great Hural (Parliament) of Mongolia, http://www.parliament.mn/en/who.

Economic Issues

Mongolia has vast mineral wealth which, if managed well, could allow it to evolve into an increasingly wealthy democracy. The country boasts reserves of coal, copper, gold, tin, and uranium, as well as reserves of molybdenum, silver, iron, phosphates, nickel, zinc, wolfram, fluorspar, and petroleum, only a small fraction of which have been developed. It also has reserves of rare earth elements, although their size is not yet known. In the short-term, however, Mongolia is grappling with declining foreign direct investment, weak mineral exports, and a resulting serious imbalance in its balance of payments. In addition, according to the World Bank, "Macro-economic and financial vulnerabilities are growing due to continuous expansionary fiscal and monetary policies reflected in significant off-budget spending and rapid credit growth."[22]

Table 1. Mongolia's Trade with Select Major Partners in 2013

(In USD millions)

Reporting Country	Imports from Mongolia	Exports to Mongolia	Total Trade	Change in Total Trade Over 2012
China	3,497	2,449	5,946	-9.79%
Russia	37	1,553	1,590	-20.43%
South Korea	27	399	426	-12.45%
Japan	19	299	319	-14.00%
United States	20	282	302	-57.30%

Source: Global Trade Atlas.

Notes: Trade figures are those reported by each country. They may differ from Mongolian trade figures.

In the medium- to long-term, Mongolia faces several existential questions related to its economic development. One is how to avoid the "natural resource curse" that has afflicted some other resource-rich countries, involving such problems as currency pressures, ballooning government budgets, corruption, and environmental degradation. Mongolia is experiencing a taste of all those issues now, but economists do not judge it yet to be in the full throes of a "natural resource curse." A second challenge is how, in a democracy, to balance the need for legal guarantees for foreign investors with the perceived need to be responsive to popular pressure to renegotiate or otherwise change the terms of contracts in order to provide the Mongolian state and public with greater rewards, particularly in extractive industries.

Another third challenge is how to overcome constraints related to Mongolia's land-locked status and limited domestic transportation networks. All goods leaving or entering Mongolia must traverse the territory of one of Mongolia's two powerful neighbors, China and Russia. (Mongolia is separated from Kazakhstan in the west by 30 miles of Russian territory.) Within Mongolia, to get to either neighbor's border, goods must currently be either trucked on mostly unpaved roads, or transported on one of just two railway lines. Mongolia's main railway is a single-track, with passing places, which runs 690 miles from the Russian border in the north to the Chinese border in the south. An eastern railway runs 148 miles from Choybalsan to the Russian border. New rail

---

[22] The World Bank Group in Mongolia, Mongolia Economic Update November 2013, http://documents.worldbank.org/curated/en/2013/11/18485265/mongolia-economic-update.

lines to the Chinese border and to the North-South rail line, are under construction, with two to the Chinese border slated for completion in 2014. (See **Figure 1** below for a map of Mongolia.)

A final existential challenge is how to stave off economic domination by neighboring China, the world's second largest economy, and lessen Mongolia's heavy dependence on Russia for energy supplies. China is currently both Mongolia's largest foreign investor and its biggest trading partner. The almost $6 billion in two-way trade between Mongolia and China is nearly four times the volume of trade between Mongolia and its second largest trading partner, Russia. (See **Table 1** below.) As of mid-2012, Chinese investment in Mongolia accounted for just under one third of total foreign direct investment (FDI) in the country.[23] Mongolia's National Security Concept document, adopted in 2010, directs the government to, "Design a strategy whereby the investment of any foreign country does not exceed one third of overall foreign investment in Mongolia."[24]

Figure 1. Map of Mongolia
Showing Railways and Major Mineral Reserves

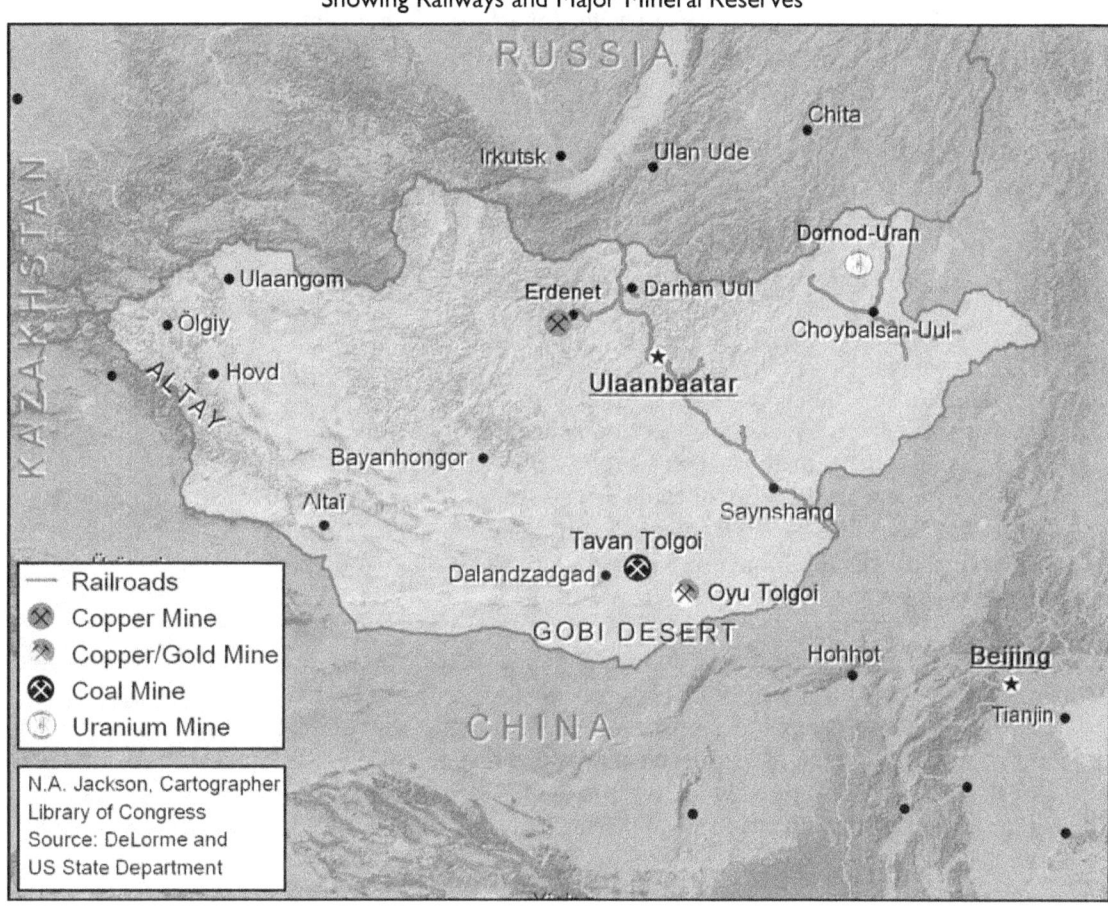

---

[23] Economic and Commercial Section of the U.S. Embassy in Ulaanbaatar, Mongolia, *2013 Mongolia Investment Climate Statement*, U.S. Department of State, January 15, 2013, http://photos.state.gov/libraries/mongolia/805999/ PDFs/mics_2013.pdf, citing statistics from the Foreign Investment Registration and Review Department of Mongolia's Ministry of Economic Development.

[24] *National Security Concept of Mongolia*, 2010. English translation provided by the Embassy of Mongolia to the United States.

Investment Climate

Mongolia has sought to attract foreign direct investment (FDI) as a way to raise capital for exploitation of its mineral resources, introduce financial and managerial expertise and new technologies, and diversify its economic partners. Government officials and Members of Parliament have periodically registered their concerns about the terms of completed investments, however, including calling for renegotiation of the terms of Mongolia's flagship foreign-invested project, a massive copper and gold mine project at Oyu Tolgoi. (See "Oyu Tolgoi Copper and Gold Deposit" below.) In addition, Mongolia's parliament has in recent years passed new laws and amended existing laws and regulations in ways that foreign investors see as sometimes curtailing previously-granted rights. In January 2013, the U.S. Embassy in Mongolia described the regulatory environment for foreign investment in Mongolia as "extremely chaotic, characterized by abrupt, non-transparent attempts to change laws."[25] As investor concerns about Mongolia's investment climate have grown, FDI in Mongolia fell in 2013 by about 55%. The Asian Development Bank attributed the sharp decline to "uncertainties" related to the regulatory framework for foreign investment, as well as to slower growth in neighboring China, the completion of the first phase of construction of the Oyu Tolgoi mine, and delays in launching the second phase of the mine project.[26] Alarmed by the drop, and responding to pressure from worried investors and from the U.S. government, Mongolia took two steps in the fall of 2013 that are credited with improving perceptions of its investment climate. They were the Mongolian parliament's October 2013 passage of a new investment law and Mongolia's September 2013 signing of a transparency agreement with the United States.

2013 Investment Law

The 2013 Mongolian Law on Investment replaced a 1993 foreign investment law and a controversial 2012 law, the Strategic Entities Foreign Investment Law of Mongolia (SEFIL). The U.S. government had raised serious concerns about SEFIL, with the U.S. Embassy in Mongolia reporting in January 2013 that investors feared SEFIL "may bar them from participating in key sectors of the Mongolian economy or force divestment of Mongolian assets and equities in the affected sectors." Because of SEFIL, the U.S. Embassy warned at the time, "both foreign and domestic investors consider Mongolia a riskier place to invest than it once was; and perhaps riskier than similar emerging markets."[27]

Under the new investment law, approvals are no longer required for foreign private investment in Mongolia, and private investments are permitted in any production or services sector not prohibited by law, with prohibited sectors limited to narcotics, gambling, pornography, and pyramid sales and marketing. Foreign state-owned companies, defined as "a legal entity in which a foreign state directly or indirectly holds more than 50 percent of the entities issued shares," are subject to restrictions that do not apply to private firms; they must seek approval for investments

---

[25] Economic and Commercial Section of the U.S. Embassy in Ulaanbaatar, Mongolia, *2013 Mongolia Investment Climate Statement*, U.S. Department of State, January 15, 2013, http://photos.state.gov/libraries/mongolia/805999/ PDFs/mics_2013.pdf.

[26] Asian Development Bank, *Asian Development Outlook 2014: Mongolia*, April 2014, http://www.adb.org/sites/ default/files/ado2014-mongolia.pdf

[27] Economic and Commercial Section of the U.S. Embassy in Ulaanbaatar, Mongolia, *2013 Mongolia Investment Climate Statement*, U.S. Department of State, January 15, 2013, http://photos.state.gov/libraries/mongolia/805999/ PDFs/mics_2013.pdf.

of more than 33% in the sectors of minerals, banking and finance, and media and telecommunications. The law also provides greater legal guarantees for investments than the laws it replaces; a stable tax environment for up to 18 years, depending on the volume and geographic location of investments; and tax and non-tax incentives for investments. In an analysis of the new law, the multinational law firm Hogan Lovells described it as "a positive step in streamlining the investment environment and creating more favorable investment conditions." The analysis noted, however, that "effective implementation is subject to further regulations" and that investors would be watching for, "consistent application of the Investment Law and a stable operating environment."[28]

U.S.-Mongolia Transparency Agreement

After years of negotiations, the United States and Mongolian governments in September 2013 signed what is formally known as the "Agreement on Transparency in Matters Related to International Trade and Investment between the United States of America and Mongolia." The United States, which pushed hard for the transparency agreement, had originally hoped to sign it before Mongolian President Elbegdorj's visit to the White House in June 2011. Although the agreement is now signed, it is still awaiting ratification by the Mongolian parliament.

The transparency agreement commits both countries to allow "a reasonable opportunity" for public comment on proposed regulations related to trade and investment, requires the text of the proposed regulations and the text of accompany rationales for the proposed regulations to be published in English at least 60 days in advance of when public comments are due, and requires both governments to accept comments solely in English. It also requires publication in English of all regulations adopted, and commits the two governments to take steps to combat bribery and corruption. A press release from the United States Trade Representative stated that the requirement that regulations be published in English "should make it easier for U.S and other foreign enterprises to do business in, and invest in, Mongolia." According to USTR, the transparency agreement with Mongolia "represents the first time that the United States has concluded a stand-alone agreement addressing transparency in matters related to international trade and investment."[29] Mongolian officials privately suggest that with the transparency agreement, the United States is seeking to hold Mongolia to a higher standard than other nations. They see the requirements for English translations as particularly onerous.

For the United States, the transparency agreement is a necessary step toward a possible future free-trade agreement (FTA) with Mongolia, the only member of the World Trade Organization that is not yet a party to any FTA. Mongolia has long sought FTA negotiations with the United States, and was disappointed that plans for such negotiations were not included in USTR's Strategic Plan for FY2013 to FY2017.[30] Observers expect Mongolia's first FTA to be with Japan.

[28] Anthony Woolley and Solongoo Bayarsaikhan, *Mongolia Revises Its Regulatory Framework for Foreign and Domestic Investment,"* Hogan Lovells, October 2013, http://www.hoganlovells.com/files/Uploads/Documents/13.11.01_F_Mongolia_revises_its_regulatory_framework_for_foreign_and_domestic_investment_October_2013.pdf. An unofficial English translation of the law is available on the website of the Mongolian Embassy to the United States, at http://www.mongolianembassy.org.au/wp-content/uploads/2013/12/MONGOLIAN-LAW-ON-INVESTMENT.pdf.

[29] United States Trade Representative, "United States, Mongolia Sign Transparency Agreement," September 24, 2014, http://www.ustr.gov/about-us/press-office/press-releases/2013/september/united-states-mongolia-sign-transparency-agreeme.

[30] Office of the U.S. Trade Representative, *Strategic Plan FY2013-FY2017,* http://www.ustr.gov/sites/default/files/USTR%20FY%202013%20-%20FY%202017%20Strategic%20Plan%20final.pdf.

Mongolia and Japan have held six rounds of Economic Partnership Agreement negotiations, with completion of the negotiations reportedly possible in 2014.

Flagship Mining Projects

Two major mineral deposits have dominated headlines about Mongolia for several years. The **Oyu Tolgoi** copper and gold deposit and the **Tavan Tolgoi** coking coal deposit, both in Mongolia's South Gobi Desert, account for a large proportion of Mongolia's hundreds of billions of dollars of untapped mineral reserves.[31] Beyond the potential profits involved, the projects have been widely viewed as important indicators of Mongolia's evolving attitude toward foreign investment. The U.S. government has expressed a particularly strong interest in Tavan Tolgoi because a U.S. company, St. Louis, Missouri-based Peabody Energy, is one of the companies competing for the rights to develop part of the deposit.

Oyu Tolgoi Copper and Gold Deposit

The Oyu Tolgoi deposit, commonly referred to as "OT," is believed to be the second largest copper deposit in the world after the Escondido copper mine in Chile. Under a multi-billion dollar 2009 deal, the deposit was to be developed jointly by Ivanhoe Mines of Canada (now known as Turquoise Hill Resources), the Australia-based Rio Tinto Group (which holds a 51% controlling stake in Turquoise Hill Resources), and the Government of Mongolia, which holds a 34% stake in the OT project. Construction of the first phase of the project began in 2010, and production began in June 2013. According to the U.S. Embassy in Mongolia's January 2013 Mongolia Investment Climate Statement, however, "doubts persist over both the GOM's [Government of Mongolia's] commitment to honoring the OT Investment Agreement (IA) and its ability to manage public expectations over mining revenues and related development."[32] The Government of Mongolia and Rio Tinto have been involved in contentious negotiations over financing of a $5.1 billion expansion of the mine, with resolution elusive. The dispute, which is being closely monitored by the foreign business community, is widely believed to have contributed to Mongolia's steep drop in foreign direct investment in 2013 and early 2014.

Tavan Tolgoi Coal Deposit

The Tavan Tolgoi deposit, commonly referred to as "TT," is believed to contain 6 billion metric tons of coal, including the world's largest untapped deposit of coking coal, which is in demand by steelmakers in China, Japan, and South Korea. In late 2008, the Mongolian parliament authorized the government to negotiate with strategic investors for rights to develop part of the deposit. In

---

[31] In Congressional testimony in March, Assistant Secretary of State Kurt Campbell said that, "According to some estimates, Mongolia has about $400 billion worth of minerals in the ground." The State Department says that figure does not include the value of Mongolia's so far largely un-surveyed rare earth minerals deposits. The same month, a Chinese coal analyst quoted in the official China Daily estimated the total value of the Tavan Tolgoi deposit alone at $300 billion. Assistant Secretary of State Kurt M. Campbell, "Asia Overview: Protecting American Interests in China and Asia," Testimony Before the House Committee on Foreign Affairs Subcommittee on Asia and the Pacific, March 31, 2011, http://www.state.gov/p/eap/rls/rm/2011/03/159450 htm; Du Juan, "Shenhua Shortlisted in Bid to Develop Mongolian Coalfield," *China Daily*, March 24, 2011.

[32] See Economic and Commercial Section of the U.S. Embassy in Ulaanbaatar, Mongolia, *2013 Mongolia Investment Climate Statement*, U.S. Department of State, January 15, 2013, http://photos.state.gov/libraries/mongolia/805999/PDFs/mics_2013.pdf

---

March 2011, the government shortlisted six bidders for rights to develop the deposit's west Tsankhi block, which has an estimated 1.2 billion tons of coal. In addition to Peabody Energy, other shortlisted bidders included a Chinese-Japanese consortium, a Korean-Russian-Japanese consortium, and firms from Brazil and Europe.[33] Whatever bidder, or combination of bidders, wins the development rights, the multi-billion dollar development of Tavan Tolgoi is expected to generate significant demand for construction and mining equipment from foreign suppliers. Development will also generate investment opportunities in such areas as power generation, water supply, and rail transport. For now, according to the U.S. Embassy in Mongolia, the delays in awarding development rights for TT are contributing to concern that the government of Mongolia "lacks both the will and the capacity to execute multiple reforms and projects."[34]

Military Engagement

Mongolia's 2011 Concept of Foreign Policy document decrees that, "In the absence of an immediate military threat, Mongolia will adopt a strategy of non-participation in any military alliance, non-use of its territory or air space against any state, non-entry, non-stationing or non-transiting of foreign troops across its territory." Mongolia has won significant goodwill from the United States and its allies for its participation in coalition operations and contributions to United Nations peacekeeping operations around the globe.

Contributions to the Wars in Afghanistan and Iraq

Mongolia was one of the first countries to join the allied coalition for the Iraq War, rotating nearly 1,200 troops through 10 consecutive deployments in Iraq between August 2003 and September 2008. Mongolian troops continue to serve in Afghanistan, where they have been deployed since 2003 in support of Operation Enduring Freedom and the International Security Assistance Force in Afghanistan. They also served with the Kosovo Force in Europe.

In an acknowledgement of the importance that the United States attaches to Mongolia's contributions to coalition operations and UN peacekeeping operations, Secretary of Defense Chuck Hagel visited Mongolia in April 2014 and, with his Mongolian counterpart, issued a "Joint Vision Statement for the U.S.-Mongolia Security Relationship." In the statement, the Department of Defense said it was "grateful for Mongolia's support," including in Afghanistan and Iraq. The statement also said the United States "commends Mongolia" for stating that if coalition forces remain in Afghanistan after 2014, it is willing to continue contributing personnel. In the statement, the United States said it welcomed Mongolian defense reform and supports improving military education for Mongolian forces.[35]

---

[33] Min-Jeong Lee, "Six in the Running for Mongolia Coal Project," *The Wall Street Journal Online*, March 7, 2011. Du Juan, "Shenhua Shortlisted in Bid to Develop Mongolian Coalfield," *China Daily*, March 24, 2011.

[34] Economic and Commercial Section of the U.S. Embassy in Ulaanbaatar, Mongolia, *2013 Mongolia Investment Climate Statement*, U.S. Department of State, January 15, 2013, http://photos.state.gov/libraries/mongolia/805999/PDFs/mics_2013.pdf.

[35] Department of Defense, *Joint Vision Statement for the U.S.-Mongolia Security Relationship*," April 10, 2014, http://www.defense.gov/pubs/FINAL-US-Mongolia-Joint-Vision-Statement-V7.pdf.

Table 2. Mongolian Participation in Coalition Missions

Mission	Dates of Participation	Total Military Personnel Deployed
Operation Iraqi Freedom (OIF)	2003-2008	1192 troops and 3 staff officers through 10 rotations
The Kosovo Force (KFOR)	2005-2007	72 troops
Operation Enduring Freedom (OEF) and the International Security Assistance Force (ISAF), Afghanistan	2003 to present	1108 troops and 351 trainers through nine rotations; 347 troops currently deployed

Source: Embassy of Mongolia in the United States communication with CRS, May 9, 2014.

The Alaska National Guard has a partnership with Mongolia under the State Partnership Program. That program pairs the National Guards of 48 states, three territories, and the District of Columbia with active and reserve forces in 68 countries around the world. Alaskan National Guard soldiers are serving as advisors for Mongolian troops in Afghanistan, and performed the same role in Iraq. Mongolia and Alaska have conducted numerous exchanges to build capacity in disaster response, health and medical care, and peacekeeping operations.[36]

Contributions to United Nations Peacekeeping Operations

Mongolia has been an active contributor of military personnel to United Nations Peacekeeping Missions. As of March 31, 2014, Mongolia had 928 troops and 10 United Nations Military Experts serving in six UN Peacekeeping Operations. Mongolia is currently the 27th largest contributor of military and police personnel to UN operations, despite its small population, with approximately 10% of Mongolia's 10,000 armed forces serving overseas in peacekeeping operations at any one time.[37] Past UN Peacekeeping missions to which Mongolia contributed personnel include the missions in Sierra Leone (UNAMSIL), Central African Republic and Chad (MINURCAT), Sudan (UNMIS), Ethiopia and Eritrea (UNMEE), and Georgia (UNOMIG).

The April 2014 U.S.-Mongolia Joint Vision Statement pledged that the United States would "continue to encourage and support Mongolia's global peacekeeping deployments and its humanitarian assistance and disaster relief capabilities."[38] The Mongolian and U.S. militaries jointly host Khaan Quest peacekeeping exercises in Mongolia each summer. The 2014 exercises, scheduled to start on June 20, 2014, are expected to involve personnel from 19 countries,

---

[36] Email from Lt. Col. Stephen Wilson, Alaska National Guard, October 22, 2010; Staff Sgt. Jim Greenhill, National Guard Bureau, *Alaska, Mongolia partnership flourishes with shared challenges*, The National Guard, February 28, 2008, http://www ng mil/news/archives/2008/02/022808-alaska.aspx; National Guard, "State Partnership Program," http://www nationalguard mil/Leadership/JointStaff/J5/InternationalAffairsDivision/StatePartnershipProgram.aspx.

[37] United Nations, "Contributors to United Nations Peacekeeping Operations: Monthly Summary of Contributions," March 31, 2014, http://www.un.org/en/peacekeeping/contributors/2014/mar14_1.pdf; United Nations, "Ranking of Military and Police Contributions to UN Operations," March 31, 2014, http://www.un.org/en/peacekeeping/contributors/2014/mar14_2.pdf.

[38] Department of Defense, *Joint Vision Statement for the U.S.-Mongolia Security Relationship,"* April 10, 2014, http://www.defense.gov/pubs/FINAL-US-Mongolia-Joint-Vision-Statement-V7.pdf.

including China.[39] The Department of Defense also supports annual Gobi Wolf exercises, aimed at improving Mongolia's disaster preparedness.

Table 3. Current Mongolian Participation in United Nations Peacekeeping Missions

As of March 31, 2014

UN Mission (Acronym)	UN Mission (Full Name)	Dates of Participation	Number of Mongolian Personnel Currently Deployed
MONUSCO	United Nations Organization Stabilization Mission in the Democratic Republic of the Congo	2002 to present	2 military observers
MINURSO	United Nations Mission for the Referendum in Western Sahara	2003 to present	4 military observers
UNAMID	African Union/United Nations Hybrid Operation in Darfur	2010 to present	70 troops
UNMISS	United Nations Mission in the Republic of South Sudan	2011 to present	858 troops; 2 staff officers
UNISFA	United Nations Interim Security Force for Abyei	2012 to present	I military observer
UNAMO	United Nations Assistance Mission in Afghanistan	2012 to present	I staff officer

Source: United Nations, "Contributors to United Nations Peacekeeping Operations: Monthly Summary of Contributions," March 31, 2014, http://www.un.org/en/peacekeeping/contributors/2014/mar14_1.pdf; United Nations, "Ranking of Military and Police Contributions to UN Operations," March 31, 2014, http://www.un.org/en/peacekeeping/contributors/2014/mar14_2.pdf.

Foreign Policy

Mongolia's official formulation of its foreign policy, the Concept of Foreign Policy, updated and approved by Mongolia's parliament in 2011, presents the country's "foreign political strategy" as consisting of five elements.

- First, Mongolia seeks to build "balanced relations and wide-ranging good neighbor cooperation" with both its immediate neighbors, Russia and China. Russia is Mongolia's largest source of energy products. Elsewhere in the Concept document, Mongolia declares that, "While seeking to develop relations and cooperation with global and regional influential states, Mongolia will avoid becoming excessively reliant or dependent on any state."

- Second, Mongolia seeks strong relations with "such Western and Eastern states and coalitions as the United States, Japan, the European Union, India, Republic of Korea and Turkey." The document presents these relationships as being within

---

[39] Email to CRS from the Embassy of Mongolia to the United States, May 8, 2014.

the framework of Mongolia's "third neighbor" policy, under which Mongolia seeks to strengthen ties with democracies that do not share borders with Mongolia, but that support its independence and sovereignty and can help to balance the influence of China and Russia.

- In Asia, Mongolia seeks to "maintain friendly bilateral relations and cooperation" with Asian neighbors, participate in multilateral cooperation, and support "policies and activities aimed at strengthening strategic stability and security cooperation in East Asia, Northeast Asia, and Central Asia."

- Mongolia pledges to "cooperate actively with the United Nations" and "support the increase of the United Nations' role and responsibilities in world governance."

- Finally, Mongolia says it will work to develop relations with other developing states, including through cooperation within the "Group of 77" developing nations at the United Nations and within the Non-Aligned Movement.

The original 1994 version of the Concept of Foreign Policy document included a focus on "reinforcing the positive legacy" of Mongolia's past relations with formerly socialist countries. That provision is missing from the 2011 version of the Concept.

Participation in International Organizations

Mongolia is an active participant in a wide range of international organizations, where it has frequently been supportive of U.S. positions. According to a State Department tally, at the fall 2013 session of 68th U.N. General Assembly, on votes that the United States considers important, Mongolia voted with the United States 83.3% of the time. By comparison, China voted with the United States on important votes 30% of the time, and Russia voted with the United States 20% of the time.[40]

Since its 1990 democratic revolution, Mongolia has joined such varied organizations and groupings as the Asian Development Bank (1991), the World Trade Organization (1997), the Association of Southeast Asian Nations (ASEAN) Regional Forum (1998), the International Criminal Court (2002), the Asia Europe Meeting (2009), and the Organization for Security and Co-Operation in Europe (2012). In 2004, it became an observer in the Shanghai Cooperation Organization, a group focused on Central Asia in which China and Russia are the dominant members, but it has so far chosen not to pursue full membership in the organization.

Mongolia has sought U.S. support for its attempts to join several other organizations. High on Mongolia's wish list is membership in the 21-member Asia-Pacific Economic Cooperation (APEC) grouping. Mongolia sees APEC membership as a way to boost its economic integration with East Asia. The group currently has a moratorium on new members, however, and if or when APEC does consider adding new members, Mongolia will likely be one among many potential candidates. Other candidates are likely to include India, Brazil, Laos, Cambodia, and Burma, the latter three being members of the Association of Southeast Asian Nations (ASEAN) that are not yet members of APEC.

---

[40] Department of State, *Voting Practices in the United Nations 2013*, March, 2014, http://www.state.gov/documents/organization/225048.pdf.

Participation in International Democracy Promotion Initiatives

Under President Elbegdorj, Mongolia has made its support for democracy a prominent part of its engagement with the international community. Examples include the following:

- From 2011 to 2013, Mongolia held the rotating chairmanship of the **Community of Democracies**, an inter-governmental coalition of democratic countries dedicated to "promoting democratic rules and strengthening democratic norms and institutions around the world."

- In May 2013, Mongolia began the process to join the **Open Government Partnership (OGP)**, a White House-backed, multilateral initiative that describes itself as having been, "launched in 2011 to provide an international platform for domestic reformers committed to making their governments more open, accountable, and responsive to citizens." Mongolia is currently developing its first action plan under the partnership. It says the plan will prioritize improving public service, increasing the transparency of public institutions, and enhancing justice and reducing corruption.[41]

- In the summer of 2014, Mongolia is scheduled to take over the rotating chairmanship of the **Freedom Online Coalition**, which describes itself as "an inter-governmental coalition committed to advancing Internet freedom—free expression, association, assembly, and privacy online—worldwide." Mongolia is scheduled to host the 5th Freedom Online Conference in its capital, Ulaanbaatar, in the spring of 2015. Coalition member states are "committed to working together diplomatically to voice concern over measures to restrict Internet freedom and support those individuals whose human rights online are curtailed." The coalition was founded in 2011 in The Hague, The Netherlands. Mongolia was one of 15 founding members. Japan is the only other Asian member.[42]

Relations with the United States

Mongolia says it considers the United States to be the most important of Mongolia's "third neighbors," countries that do not share borders with Mongolia, but that Mongolia looks to for support of its independence and sovereignty and for balance against the influence of China and Russia. The United States established diplomatic relations with Mongolia in January 1987, after the rise of Mikhail Gorbachev in the Soviet Union produced a cautious warming in Soviet-United States relations. In that context, Moscow, which had previously objected to diplomatic relations between Mongolia and the United States, softened its position. The United States Embassy in Mongolia opened in September, 1988. Washington at that time saw the post as a useful vantage point for monitoring the Sino-Soviet relationship and the new policies of *glasnost* and *perestroika*

---

[41] Open Government Partnership website, http://www.opengovpartnership.org/ and http://www.opengovpartnership.org/country/mongolia, accessed June 5, 2014. See also, The White House Office of the Press Secretary, "Fact Sheet: The Open Government Partnership," September 20, 2011, http://www.whitehouse.gov/the-press-office/2011/09/20/fact-sheet-open-government-partnership.

[42] E. Dari, "Mongolia to Chair Online Freedom Coalition," *The UB Post*, April 30, 2014, http://ubpost.mongolnews mn/?p=8901; Website of the Freedom Online Coalition, http://www freedomonline.ee/about-us/Freedom-online-coalition; Freedom Online Coalition Chair's Summary, April 28-29, 2014, http://www freedomonline.ee/sites/www freedomonline.ee/files/docs/FOC%20Chair's%20Summary%2009%2005%202014.pdf.

---

emanating from Moscow. From the embassy, however, American diplomats found themselves afforded an up-close view of Mongolia's 1990 democratic revolution.[43]

Today, the United States and Mongolia have declared themselves to be in a "comprehensive partnership based on common values and shared strategic interests," language included in the U.S.-Mongolia Joint Statement issued during President Elbegdorj's visit to the United States in 2011. The Joint Statement pronounced the two countries united in their interest in "protecting and promoting freedom, democracy and human rights worldwide," in their commitment to "promoting a peaceful, stable and prosperous Asia-Pacific region," and in their desire to work together "to address their shared economic, security and development interests though multi-lateral institutions in the Asia-Pacific, the United Nations, and elsewhere. The statement highlighted U.S. gratitude to Mongolia for its participation in the international coalition in Afghanistan, and for its role in UN Peacekeeping Operations, and Mongolian gratitude to the United States for support provided under its 2008-2013 Millennium Challenge Corporation Compact. The two sides pledged "to strengthen trade, investment and people-to-people ties."[44]

High-level Visits

A sign of the United States' strong support for Mongolia's young democracy is the fact that Mongolia has hosted visits by multiple senior U.S. executive branch officials and Congressional leaders since Mongolia's democratic transition in 1990. See **Table 4** below for a list of executive branch visitors. House Speaker Dennis Hastert visited in 2005 and House Minority Leader John Boehner in 2009. Members of Congress have also visited Mongolia under the auspices of the House Democracy Partnership.

Table 4. Visits to Mongolia by Senior U.S. Executive Branch Officials
Since Mongolia's 1990 Democratic Revolution

Offices	Names	Year of Visit
President	George W. Bush	2005
Vice-President	Joe Biden	2011
First Ladies	Hillary Clinton	1995
	Laura Bush	2005
Secretaries of State	James Baker	1990 and 1991
	Madeleine Albright	1998
	Condoleeza Rice	2005
	Hillary Clinton	2012

---

[43] For a detailed account of the negotiations leading up to the establishment of diplomatic relations, and of the early years of U.S.-Mongolian relations, see Alicia Campi and R. Baasan, *The Impact of China and Russia on United States-Mongolian Political Relations in the Twentieth Century* (The Edwin Mellen Press, 2009), pp. 375-397. Campi was a State Department official on temporary assignment at the U.S. Embassy in Ulaanbaatar at the time of the 1990 democratic revolution.

[44] The White House, "U.S.-Mongolia Joint Statement," June 16, 2011, http://www.whitehouse.gov/the-press-office/2011/06/16/us-mongolia-joint-statement.

Offices	Names	Year of Visit
Secretaries of Defense	Donald Rumsfeld	2005
	Chuck Hagel	2014
Secretary of Agriculture (leading Presidential delegation)	Mike Johanns	2006

Source: Media reports and U.S. government websites.

Table 5. Visits to the United States by Senior Mongolian Officials
Since Mongolia's 1990 Democratic Revolution

Offices	Names	Year of Visit
Presidents	Punsalmaagiyn Ochirbat	1991
	Natsagiin Bagabandi	2004
	Nambaryn Enkhbayar	2007
	Tsakhiagiin Elbegdorj	2011
Prime Ministers	Dash Byambasuren	1991
	Puntsag Jasrai	1993
	Mendsaikhan Enkhsaikhan	1996
	Ryenchinnyam Amarjargal	1999
	Nambaryn Enkhbayar	2001
	Sanjaasuren Bayar	2008
	Sukhbaatar Batbold	2011
Chairmen of the State Great Hural	Radnaasumberel Gonchigdorj	1998
	Damdin Demberel	2011
	Zandaakhuu Enkhbold	2013
Ministers of Foreign Affairs	Tserenpil Gombosuren	1994
	Ryenchinnyam Amarjargal	1998
	Nyam-Osor Tuya	2000
	Luvsan Erdenechuluun	2000
	Sukhbaatar Batbold	2009
Minister of Defense	Luvsanvandan Bold	2011

Source: Embassy of Mongolia to the United States; U.S. government websites and media reports.

Major Bilateral Agreements

The Clinton Administration concluded a Bilateral Investment Treaty with Mongolia in 1994; the Senate ratified it in 1996 (Senate Treaty Doc. 104-10), and it went into effect on January 1, 1997. The 106th Congress extended permanent normal trade relations to Mongolia in 1999, and the George W. Bush Administration concluded a Trade and Investment Framework Agreement with Mongolia in 2004. Two countries concluded a memorandum of understanding on cooperation in peaceful uses of nuclear energy in 2010, and signed an Agreement on Transparency in Matters

Related to International Trade and Investment in 2013. (See "U.S.-Mongolia Transparency Agreement" above.)

U.S. Assistance to Mongolia

The United States provided $9.21 million in bilateral foreign assistance to Mongolia in FY2013, and an estimated $8.49 million in FY2014. For FY2015, the State Department has requested $9.4 million in bilateral foreign assistance, a $910,000 increase from the FY2014 estimate.[45] (See **Table 6** below.)

Nearly two-thirds of the State Department's FY2015 request for Mongolia is in the form of development assistance. Reflecting high rates of economic growth in Mongolia in recent years, USAID is transitioning to a "legacy program" in Mongolia, or what the agency calls "an economic partnership based on shared commercial interests and investment," which will likely result in lower budget requests in future years. USAID and the Mongolian government are still negotiating the details of the legacy program, but the State Department says it will aim to "help build the capacity of the government to manage revenues generated from the extractive industries by strengthening the public administration system."[46]

Defense cooperation has been a major component of the U.S.-Mongolian relationship. Appropriations for Foreign Military Financing (FMF) for Mongolia dropped from $4.5 million in FY2010 to an estimated $2.4 million in FY2014. The Administration's FY2015 budget request further drops FMF for Mongolia to $2 million. FMF from the United States supports Mongolia's peacekeeping capacity, including communications equipment, "personal protective equipment," vehicles, and logistics equipment for Mongolian peacekeeping forces.

Table 6. U.S. Bilateral Foreign Assistance to Mongolia FY2009-FY2012

(In USD thousands)

	FY2013 Actual	FY2014 Estimate	FY2015 Request
Development Assistance	5,159	5,000	6,000
Foreign Military Financing (FMF)	3,048	2,400	2,000
International Military Education and Training (IMET)	755	850	1,150
Nonproliferation, Antiterrorism, Demining and Related Programs	250	240	250
TOTAL	9,212	8,490	9,400

[45] U.S. Department of State, *FY 2015Congressional Budget Justification - Foreign Operations: Appendix 3: Regional Perspectives*, April 18, 2014, http://www.state.gov/documents/organization/224070.pdf.

[46] U.S. Department of State, *FY 2015Congressional Budget Justification - Foreign Operations: Appendix 3: Regional Perspectives*, p. 277, April 18, 2014, http://www.state.gov/documents/organization/224070.pdf.

Source: U.S. Department of State, *FY 2012 Congressional Budget Justification - Foreign Operations*, April 11, 2011, http://www.state.gov/f/releases/iab/fy2012cbj/pdf/index.htm; U.S. Department of State, *FY 2011 Congressional Budget Justification - Foreign Operations*, March 2010, http://www.state.gov/documents/organization/137937.pdf.

Notes: Country totals for foreign assistance under the continuing resolution, H.R. 1473, P.L. 112-10, signed into law on April 15, 2011, have not yet been finalized.

The FY2015 budget request increases funding for International Military Education and Training (IMET) for Mongolia. IMET funds support professional military education and technical training, including English-language training for Mongolia's forces, and has supported the enrollment of Mongolian officers in such institutions as the U.S. National Defense University, the Army War College and command and staff colleges of the U.S. services. The State Department notes that IMET graduates led all ten Mongolian units that served in Iraq and have led all units deployed to Afghanistan.

Millennium Challenge Corporation Compact

The United States' $284.9 million Millennium Challenge Compact with Mongolia, signed in 2007, expired in September 2013. Included in the compact were five projects to build infrastructure, strengthen vocational education for the unemployed and marginally employed, address environmental challenges, strengthen property rights, and support public health. The infrastructure project, the North-South Road Project, involved construction of a 110 mile-long road that was to complete the last unpaved section of highway connecting Europe with East Asia.[47] Countries eligible for Millennium Challenge Corporation (MCC) support must perform above the median in their peer group in "ruling justly, investing in people, and encouraging economic freedom."[48]

Mongolia sought but was not selected for a second MCC compact at the MCC's board's December 2013 meeting. Because the World Bank now categorizes Mongolia as a "Low Middle Income Country," it faces stiffer competition for more limited MCC funds.

Select U.S. Government Programs in Mongolia

The Peace Corps currently has 111 volunteers assigned to Mongolia. They are training Mongolian English teachers and teaching English, as well as working in the areas of community-based health, community youth development, and community and economic development. More than 1050 Peace Corps volunteers have served in Mongolia since 1991.[49]

The Department of Commerce's International Trade Administration (ITA) organizes capacity building programs for Mongolian officials on trade issues and holds an annual United States-Mongolia Business Forum in the United States.[50]

---

[47] Ibid and Millennium Challenge Corporation, Mongolia: Roads, Energy, Vocational Training, Health and Land Tenure," http://www.mcc.gov/documents/reports/countrybrief-2013002144801-mongolia.pdf.

[48] Millennium Challenge Corporation, *Mongolia Compact*, http://www.mcc.gov/pages/countries/program/mongolia-compact.

[49] For more information, see *Peace Corps: Mongolia,* http://www.peacecorps.gov/volunteer/learn/wherepc/asia/mongolia/ and Peace *Peace Corps Mongolia*, http://mongolia.peacecorps.gov/projects.php.

[50] International Trade Administration, "Under Secretaryof Commerce for International Trade Francisco Sanchez Arrives in Mongolia to Advance Commercial Relationship," April 4, 2013, http://trade.gov/press/press-releases/2013/ (continued...)

The Department of the Treasury's Office of Technical Assistance (OTA) has a resident advisor stationed in Mongolia, assigned to Mongolia's Ministry of Finance. He has been advising the Ministry on "domestic and sovereign bond sales, cash forecasting and development of the sovereign wealth fund."[51]

Relations with Russia[52]

Mongolia was a satellite state of the Soviet Union from 1921 until 1990. The relationship entailed one-party rule under the communist Mongolian People's Revolutionary Party, a foreign policy dictated by the Soviet Union, state-owned industry, collectivized livestock herding, suppression of Mongolia's Tibetan Buddhist religion, and rounds of political purges. With military backing from the Soviet Union, however, Mongolia was able to exist as a state in its own right, with its own membership in the United Nations (gained in 1961) and in the Council for Mutual Economic Assistance (Comecon), the economic organization for Soviet bloc countries (gained in 1962). Mongolians had opportunities to pursue advanced studies in the Soviet Union and Eastern Europe. The Soviet Union partnered with Mongolia to build the country's main rail line, a single track running from the Russian border in the north to the Chinese border in the south. The Soviet Union also partnered with Mongolia to develop the Erdenet copper and molybdenum mine, which opened in 1978 and was until recently Mongolia's top export earner.

With Mongolia's 1990 democratic revolution and the collapse of the Soviet Union, Russia cut off aid, withdrew its last troops from Mongolia in 1992, and began to demand the repayment of aid the Soviet Union had given to Mongolia between 1946 and 1990. The debt remained a thorn in bilateral relations until December 2010, when the two countries declared a final settlement of the dispute.

In recent years, Mongolia has sought to bolster ties with Russia, in part to balance China's influence. The two countries declared themselves "strategic partners" in 2005. Mongolia remains dependent on Russia for energy products, particularly diesel, as well as for access to international markets. Russia has been eager to cooperate with Mongolia in development of Mongolia's uranium resources. The U.S. government is more comfortable with Russian involvement in Mongolian's uranium sector than with the involvement of other players with less developed protocols for management of uranium.

The Russian government continues to be a joint owner of Mongolia's railway, through the state-owned company JSC Russian Railways, and of the Erdenet copper mine. The two countries have discussed further cooperation in railway infrastructure. Russian firms are also involved in the bidding for the right to develop the Tavan Tolgoi coal deposit, and have expressed interest in

---

(...continued)

under-secretary-of-commerce-for-international-trade-francisco-sanchez-arrives-in-mongolia-to-advance-commercial-relationship-040413.asp.

[51] Department of the Treasury, "Office of Technical Assistance Mission Statement," http://www.treasuryota.us/; Mongolia Projects and Investment Summit, "Daniel Patrick O'Connell, Resident Debt Advisor for Mongolia, U.S. Department of the Treasury c/o Mongolia Ministry of Finance," http://mongoliainvestmentsummit.com/hongkong/daniel-patrick-oconnell-resident-debt-advisor-for-mongolia-u-s-department-of-the-treasury-co-mongolia-ministry-of-finance/.

[52] Drawn from Alan J.K. Sanders, *Historical Dictionary of Mongolia*, 3rd ed. (The Scarecrow Press, Inc., 2010), pp. 616-625.

other investment opportunities related to the Tavan Tolgoi project. Military ties are warming, too. In November 2008, Mongolia and Russia held their first joint military exercises in Mongolia since the departure of the last Russian troops from Mongolian soil in 1992.

Relations with China

Mongolia is committed to "balanced" relations with both Russia and China. China has become by far Mongolia's largest trading partner, as well as its largest source of foreign investment. The two countries formally embraced a "good neighborly partnership of mutual trust" in 2003,[53] and have engaged in bilateral peacekeeping exercises. The "Peacekeeping Mission 2009," held in China in the summer of 2009, was the first joint peacekeeping exercise China had held with another country, as well as the first joint military training between the two countries.[54]

Yet each side remains wary of the other. Mongolia worries about economic domination by China. The 2012 Strategic Entities Foreign Investment Law of Mongolia (SEFIL) is reported to have been enacted, at least in part, to block the acquisition of a Mongolian coal mining firm by a state-owned Chinese aluminum firm, Chalco.[55] The 2013Mongolian Law on Investment that replaced it maintained restrictions on state-owned enterprises, a category that includes many of the biggest Chinese firms seeking to invest in Mongolia. Being sparsely populated, Mongolia also worries about being overrun by workers and immigrants from China, including from China's Inner Mongolia Autonomous Region, which has a larger ethnic Mongolian population than the country of Mongolia itself.

Culturally, Mongolia has been ranked by China's efforts to register elements of traditional Mongolian culture as Chinese with the United Nations Educational, Scientific, and Cultural Organization (UNESCO).[56] For its part, China has lingering concerns about the potential for a "pan-Mongol" movement, linking Mongolians on both sides of the Chinese-Mongolian border, to undermine stability in Inner Mongolia. Beijing is also deeply uncomfortable with Mongolia's close ties to Tibet's exiled spiritual leader, the Dalai Lama, whom China blames for resistance to Chinese control in Tibet and Tibetan areas of China.

Ties to Tibetan Buddhism and the Dalai Lama

Mongolia and Tibet have a long shared history. In 1578, a Mongolian ruler, Altyn Khan, originated the title of the Dalai Lama, the title held by the spiritual leader of Tibet. Altyn Khan conferred the title—"Dalai" means "Oceanic" in Mongolian—on a Tibetan Buddhist leader who was the third incarnation of his Gelugpa sect's reincarnation line. The man became the 3rd Dalai Lama and his two predecessors retroactively became the 1st and 2nd Dalai Lamas. After the 3rd Dalai Lama's death, a great-grandson of Altyn Khan was identified as his reincarnation,

---

[53] Website of the Ministry of Foreign Affairs of the People's Republic of China, "Mongolia," http://www.fmprc.gov/ cn/chn/pds/gjhdq/gj/yz/1206_21/.

[54] "China, Mongolia launch joint peacekeeping exercise," *Xinhua*, June 29, 2009.

[55] Clement Huaweilang Dai and David Tyler Gibson, "Minegolia Part I: China and Mongolia's Mining Boom," The Wilson Center China Environment Forum, June 21, 2013.

[56] Mongolia objected in 2010, for example, to UNESCO's listing of Khoomii, the traditional Mongolian art of throat singing, as an intangible cultural heritage of China. Jargal Byambasuren, "Mongolian throat singers defend tradition against China," *Reuters*, February 11, 2010.

becoming the 4th Dalai Lama and the only Mongolian Dalai Lama in the history of the institution.[57]

For centuries, Tibetan Buddhism, and specifically the Dalai Lama's Gelugpa order of Tibetan Buddhism, was the predominant religion in Mongolia. Close religious ties were a backdrop to Mongolia and Tibet's decision in 1913 to sign a treaty declaring themselves free from Manchu Chinese rule and recognizing each other as independent states. Despite decades of religious suppression during the Soviet era, Tibetan Buddhism has revived in Mongolia in the democratic era. According to the Pew Forum on Religion and Public Life, 55.1 percent of Mongolia's population is Buddhist, making Mongolia one of seven nations in the world with Buddhist majorities.[58] Mongolian monks train in the monasteries of the exile Tibetan movement in India, and the current incarnation of the Dalai Lama, the 14th, has made six ostensibly private visits to Mongolia since the 1990 democratic revolution, in 1991, 1994, 1995, 2002, and 2006, and 2011, despite objections from China. (The 14th Dalai Lama first visited Mongolia in 1979.) In November 2002, in a powerful show of displeasure with Mongolia for hosting the Dalai Lama, China closed its side of the Chinese-Mongolian rail border for 36 hours, highlighting Mongolia's geographic dependence on China's goodwill.[59] Mongolians are reportedly deeply concerned about signals that China intends to control the reincarnation process for the current Dalai Lama, with many Mongolians rejecting the idea that Beijing should be permitted to select their spiritual leader.

Relations with Japan

Japan is one of Mongolia's leading "third neighbors," countries that do not share geographic borders with Mongolia but to which Mongolia looks for diplomatic and other forms of support. Mongolia and Japan established diplomatic relations in 1972, but the relationship remained largely inactive until 1990. Shortly after the democratic revolution, the two countries exchanged prime ministerial visits and Japan organized a series of conferences for aid donors to Mongolia. Japan remains Mongolia's largest donor, having provided Mongolia with cumulative bilateral assistance of $2.13 billion (216,578 million yen) as of March 2013.[60]The Japanese government has expressed frustration, however, that its companies have struggled to gain a foothold in Mongolia.

Mongolia and Japan announced a "comprehensive partnership" in 1998, and committed in 2010 to building a "strategic partnership." They entered into negotiations over a free trade zone, the Japan-Mongolia Economic Partnership Agreement, in 2012. Negotiations remain ongoing. Mongolia has pledged support for Japan's campaign for a permanent seat on the U.N. Security Council, a campaign that China opposes.[61]

---

[57] Melvyn C. Goldstein, *The Snow Lion and the Dragon: China, Tibet, and the Dalai Lama*, University of California Press, 1977, pp. 7-8.

[58] The world's other six majority Buddhist nations are Cambodia, Thailand, Burma, Bhutan, Sri Lanka, and Laos. The Pew Forum on Religion & Public Life, *The Global Religious Landscape: A Report on the Size and Distribution of the World's Major Religious Groups as of 2010*, December 2012, http://www.pewforum.org/files/2014/01/global-religion-full.pdf.

[59] Alan J.K. Sanders, *Historical Dictionary of Mongolia*, 3rd ed. (The Scarecrow Press, Inc., 2010), pp. 686-689; 156.

[60] Ministry of Foreign Affairs of Japan, Mongolia: Basic Data, http://www mofa.go.jp/region/asia-paci/mongolia/data html.

[61] Alan J.K. Sanders, *Historical Dictionary of Mongolia*, 3rd ed. (The Scarecrow Press, Inc., 2010), pp. 358-360.

Relations with the Koreas

Mongolians have strong historical ties with the Korean peninsula, with many Koreans believing their ancestors came from Mongolia. In 1948, when Mongolia was a satellite of the Soviet Union, it was just the second country to recognize the new Democratic People's Republic of Korea (North Korea), after the Soviet Union itself. In 1990, one of Mongolia's first foreign policy acts after the democratic revolution was to establish diplomatic relations with the Republic of Korea (South Korea). Mongolia, like China and Russia, therefore has official relations with both Koreas.

Mongolia sees South Korea as a model for free-market economic development and a source of technology and capital. It is also reportedly home to as many as one fifth of Mongolians living abroad, with 32,206 Mongolians living long-term in South Korea as of 2008.[62] South Korea has become a major Mongolian trading partner, although two-way trade figures are dwarfed by those for Mongolia's trade with China and Russia. Mongolia deems South Korea to be one of its "third neighbors," countries that do not share borders with Mongolia but share close ties with it.

With encouragement from Western governments, starting in 1996, a succession of Mongolian governments has reached out to North Korea, seeking to reduce the country's isolation and encourage it to engage with multilateral efforts to address security issues on the Korean peninsula. Mongolia is also keenly interested in securing access to North Korea's Rajin-Sonbong port, which would reduce Mongolia's reliance on the Chinese port of Tianjin, although Mongolian goods would still need to travel through Chinese or Russian territory to reach Rajin-Sonbong.

North Korea's response to Mongolia's overtures has been mixed. High-level contacts, which had dropped off after Mongolia's 1990 democratic revolution, resumed in 1998. A year later, however, Mongolia expressed support for South Korea's "Sunshine" policy, leading an angry North Korea to shutter its embassy in the Mongolian capital, Ulaanbaatar. When the embassy re-opened in 2004, a North Korean official suggested establishing joint farm operations in several Mongolian provinces. Several thousand North Korean agricultural experts and workers are now estimated to be employed on farms in Mongolia. Mongolian officials hope that North Korean workers exposed to life in democratic Mongolia might help change mindsets back in North Korea after their return, although some also worry that North Korean workers' earnings may be lining the pockets of the North Korean elite. Mongolia's role as a transit stop for North Korean refugees arriving from China has been a sensitive issue in Mongolian-North Korean relations. Mongolia's former ambassador to the United States has been quoted as saying that between 1999 and 2003, more than 600 North Koreans who entered Mongolia from China were re-settled in South Korea.[63]

Mongolian President Elbegdorj visited Pyongyang in October 2013, becoming the first head of state to visit since Kim Jong Un succeeded his father as North Korea's top leader in December 2011. Elbegdorj gave a speech at Kim Il Sung University on his last day in the country entitled, "It is the Human Desire to Live Free That Is an Eternal Power." The speech including the

---

[62] The one fifth statistic is from Migeddorj Batchimeg, "Mongolia's DPRK Policy: Engaging North Korea," *Asian Survey*, vol. 46, no. 2 (March/April 2006), pp. 282. The number of Mongolians living in South Korea is from the website of the Ministry of Foreign Affairs and Trade of the Republic of Korea, http://www.mofat.go.kr/english/regions/asia/20070802/1_292.jsp?board=board&boardid=&key=1.

[63] Migeddorj Batchimeg, "Mongolia's DPRK Policy: Engaging North Korea," *Asian Survey*, vol. 46, no. 2 (March/April 2006), pp. 275-297.

memorable line, "No tyranny last forever." In a note on his website, Elbegdorj stated that the North Korean side proposed the lecture topic, although the North Korean government advised him to avoid use of the words "democracy" and "market economy."[64] Elbegdorj did not meet Kim Jong Un on his trip; North Korea instead arranged for him to meet with its number two leader, Kim Yong Nam. In March 2014, Mongolia hosted a reunion between the North Korea-based daughter of a Japanese woman abducted by North Korea in 1977 and her Japanese grandparents.[65]

Nuclear-Weapons-Free Status

Mongolia unilaterally declared itself a nuclear-weapon-free zone (NWFZ) in 1992, soon after the 1990 democratic revolution, and has sought to establish an international legal basis for the status ever since. The Law of Mongolia on Its Nuclear-Weapon-Free Status, which was adopted in 1992 and entered into force in 2000, makes it illegal to develop, manufacture, possess, control, station, transport, test, or use nuclear weapons on Mongolian territory. It also makes it illegal to "dump or dispose nuclear weapons grade radioactive material or nuclear waste" on Mongolian territory.[66] Mongolia's declaration was significant in that it signaled a rejection of nuclear weapons by a country with perhaps the world's second largest inferred reserves of uranium, an essential fuel for the nuclear power industry that can also be used to make nuclear weapons.[67] Mongolia's Ambassador to the International Atomic Energy Agency (IAEA), Jargalsaikhany Enkhsaikhan, explained in a 2010 interview that a major impetus for the declaration was Mongolia's experiences during the Sino-Soviet split of the 1960s, when the threat of nuclear war between the two giants loomed large and Mongolia, as a Soviet satellite state with Soviet troops and missiles on its territory, found itself uncomfortably on the Russian front line.[68]

The Permanent Five (P-5) members of the U.N. Security Council – Britain, China, France, Russia, and the United States – welcomed Mongolia's NWFZ declaration, but until 2012 stopped short of extending it formal recognition. In his 2010 interview, Ambassador Enkhsaikhan attributed the P-5's reluctance to a concern that recognizing Mongolia's single-state NWFZ, "would reduce or undermine the incentive for establishing traditional (i.e., group) NWFZs and set a precedent for others to follow suit."[69] Mongolia had no choice but to declare a single-state NWFZ, however, because its only contiguous neighbors are both nuclear powers. In September 2012, the P-5 countries signed parallel political declarations which, according to the State Department, "affirmed their intent to respect Mongolia's nuclear-weapon-free status and not to contribute to any act that would violate it." The P-5 have also supported seven UN General Assembly resolutions since 1992 inviting member states to support Mongolia's nuclear-weapon-free status.[70]

---

[64] The Office of the President of Mongolia, *Lecture by President Tsakhiagiin Elbegdorj at Kim Il Sung University, North Korea," October 30, 2013,* http://www.president.mn/eng/newsCenter/viewNews.php?newsId=1008.

[65] Martin Fackler, "Years After Abduction by North Korea, a Reunion," *The New York Times,* March 16, 2014.

[66] "Law of Mongolia on its Nuclear-Weapon-Free Status," declared September 25, 1992, Inventory of International Nonproliferation Organizations and Regimes, Center for Nonproliferation Studies.

[67] Susan Wacaster, *2009 Minerals Yearbook: The Mineral Industry of Mongolia,* United States Geological Survey, Washington, D.C., February 2011, p. 18.3, http://minerals.usgs.gov/minerals/pubs/country/2009/myb3-2009-mg.pdf.

[68] Giovanni Verlini, "Keeping Nuclear Weapons Out: Ambassador Jargalsaikhany Enkhsaikhan spoke with the Bulletin's Giovanni Verlini about Mongolia's nuclear-weapon-free zone," *IAEA Bulletin,* vol. 51-2 (April 2010), p. 44-47.

[69] Ibid.

[70] U.S. Department of State, "Five Permanent UN Representatives Support Mongolia's Nuclear Weapon-Free Status," (continued...)

Appendix A. Select Legislation on Mongolia

Table A-1. Select Legislation Related to Mongolia from the 102nd Congress to the Present

(Listed in reverse chronological order, with most recent first)

Bill Number	Legislative Sponsor	Date Agreed To	Title/Description
S.Res. 208 (112th Congress)	Kerry	June 15, 2011	Expressing the sense of the Senate regarding Mongolian President Tsakhiagiin Elbegdorj's visit to Washington, D.C., and its support for the growing partnership between the United States and Mongolia.
S.Res. 192 (111th Congress)	Kerry	June 18, 2009	Expressing the sense of the Senate regarding supporting democracy and economic development in Mongolia and expanding relations between the United States and Mongolia.
P.L. 110-161 (H.R. 2764)	Lowey	December 26, 2007	Consolidated Appropriations Act, 2008 Stated that in FY2008, funds available to the Department of Defense could be expended for crating, packing, handling, and transportation of excess defense articles to Mongolia, among other nations.
S.Res. 352 (110th Congress)	Murkowski	October 18, 2007	Expressing the sense of the Senate regarding the 20th anniversary of United States-Mongolia relations.
H.Res. 828 (109th Congress)	Pitts	June 7, 2006	Commending the people of Mongolia, on the 800th anniversary of Mongolian statehood, for building strong, democratic institutions, and expressing the support of the House of Representatives for efforts by the United States to continue to strengthen its partnership with that country.
P.L. 109-102 (H.R. 3057)	Kolbe	November 14, 2005	Foreign Operations, Export Financing, and Related Programs Appropriations Act, 2006 Stated that in FY2006, funds available to the Department of Defense could be expended for crating, packing, handling, and transportation of excess defense articles to Mongolia, among other nations.
P.L. 108-447 (H.R. 4818)	Kolbe	December 8, 2004	Consolidated Appropriations Act, 2005 Stated that in FY2005, funds available to the Department of Defense could be expended for crating, packing, handling, and transportation of excess defense articles to Mongolia, among other nations.

(...continued)

September 18, 2012, http://www.state.gov/r/pa/prs/ps/2012/09/197873 htm.

Bill Number	Legislative Sponsor	Date Agreed To	Title/Description
P.L. 107-228 (H.R. 1646)	Hyde	September 30, 2002	Foreign Relations Authorization Act, Fiscal Year 2003
			Stated that in FY2003, funds available to the Department of Defense could be expended for crating, packing, handling, and transportation of excess defense articles to Mongolia, among other nations. Also stated that it was the sense of the Congress that the authority provided "should be utilized only for those countries demonstrating a genuine commitment to democracy and human rights."
P.L. 107-115 (H.R. 2506)	Kolbe	January 10, 2002	Foreign Operations, Export Financing, and Related Programs Appropriations Act, 2002
			Stated that in FY2002 and 2003, funds available to the Department of Defense could be expended for crating, packing, handling, and transportation of excess defense articles to Mongolia, among other nations.
P.L. 106-429 (H.R. 4811)	Callahan	November 6, 2000	Foreign Operations, Export Financing, and Related Programs Appropriations Act, 2001
			Made available to Mongolia not less than $12 million in Economic Support Fund appropriations.
P.L. 106-280 (H.R. 4919)	Gilman	October 6, 2000	Security Assistance Act of 2000
			Stated that funds available to the Department of Defense could be expended for crating, packing, handling, and transportation of excess defense articles to Mongolia.
P.L. 106-113 (H.R. 3194)	Istook	November 29, 1999	Consolidated Appropriations Act, 2000
			Made available to Mongolia not less than $6 million in bilateral economic assistance.
P.L. 106-36 (H.R. 435)	Archer	June 25, 1999	Miscellaneous Trade and Technical Corrections Act of 1999
			Extended permanent normal trade relations treatment to the products of Mongolia.
P.L. 105-277 (H.R. 4328)	Wolf	October 21, 1998	Omnibus Consolidated and Emergency Supplemental Appropriations Act, 1999
			Stated that bilateral economic assistance funds should be made available for Mongolia at a level at least equivalent to the level provided in FY1998.
P.L. 105-118 (H.R. 2159)	Callahan	November 26, 1997	Foreign Operations, Export Financing, and Related Programs Appropriations Act, 1998
			Made bilateral economic assistance funds available to Mongolia.

Bill Number	Legislative Sponsor	Date Agreed To	Title/Description
P.L. 104-208 (H.R. 3610)	Young	September 30, 1996	Omnibus Consolidated Appropriations Act, 1997. Made $10 million in bilateral economic assistance available only for assistance to Mongolia, of which not less than $6 million was to be available only for the Mongolian energy sector.
S.Res. 276 (104th Congress)	Robb	September 6, 1996	Congratulating the people of Mongolia on embracing democracy in Mongolia through their participation in the parliamentary elections held on June 30, 1996.
P.L. 104-107 (H.R. 1868)	Callahan	February 12, 1996	Foreign Operations, Export Financing, and Related Programs Appropriations Act, 1996. Made available to Mongolia funds appropriated for assistance for the new independent states of the former Soviet Union.
H.Res. 158 (104th Congress)	Bereuter	September 18, 1995	Congratulating the people of Mongolia on the 5th anniversary of the first democratic multiparty elections held in Mongolia on July 29, 1990.
P.L. 103-306 H.R. 4426	Obey	August 23, 1994	Foreign Operations, Export Financing, and Related Programs Appropriations Act, 1995. Made available to Mongolia funds appropriated for assistance for the new independent states of the former Soviet Union.
P.L. 102-157 (H.J.Res. 281)	Gephardt	November 13, 1991	Approving the extension of nondiscriminatory treatment with respect to the products of the Mongolian People's Republic.
S.Con.Res. 21 (102nd Congress)	Cranston	October 17, 1991	A concurrent resolution commending the people of Mongolia on their first multi-party elections.

Source: Legislative Information System of the U.S. Congress.

Appendix B. Results of Mongolian Elections 1992-Present

Table B-1. Results of Direct Presidential Elections

Date	Winning Candidate	Party	Percentage of Vote Won
June 6, 1993	Punsalmaagiin Ochirbat	Mongolian National Democratic Party and Mongolian Social Democratic Party	57.8
May 18, 1997	Natsagiin Bagabandi	Mongolian People's Revolutionary Party	60.8
May 20, 2001	Natsagiin Bagabandi	Mongolian People's Revolutionary Party	57.95
May 22, 2005	Nambaryn Enkhbayar	Mongolian People's Revolutionary Party	53
May 24, 2009	Tsakhiagiin Elbegdorj	Democratic Party	51.21
June 26, 2013	Tsakhiagiin Elbegdorj	Democratic Party	50.23

Source: For elections from 1993 to 2009, Alan J.K. Sanders, *Historical Dictionary of Mongolia*, 3rd ed. (The Scarecrow Press, Inc., 2010), pp. 585-586. For 2013 election, ElectionGuide: Democracy Assistance & Election News, International Foundation for Electoral Systems, http://www.electionguide.org/countries/id/144/.

Notes: In September 1990, prior to passage of the 1992 democratic constitution, Mongolia's then parliament elected Ochirbat president for the first time as the candidate of the Mongolian People's Revolutionary Party (MPRP). The MPRP declined to select him as its candidate for the 1993 direct presidential election, so Ochirbat ran instead as the candidate of the Mongolian National Democratic Party and the Mongolian Social Democratic Party. He defeated the MPRP's candidate, 57.8% to 38.7%. (See Alan J.K. Sanders, *Historical Dictionary of Mongolia*, 3rd ed. (The Scarecrow Press, Inc., 2010), pp. 546-547.

Table B-2. Results of Direct Parliamentary Elections 1992-Present

The State Great Hural has 76 Seats. Majority Party or Coalition is in Bold Type.

Date	Breakdown of Seats	Prime Ministers
June 28, 1992	**Mongolian People's Revolutionary Party (MPRP): 70 seats**	Puntsagiin Jasrai (7/20/1992-7/19/1996)
	Democratic Union Coalition (the Mongolian Democratic Party, Mongolian National Progressive Party, and the Mongolian United Party): 4 seats	
	Mongolian Social Democratic Party (MSDP): 1 seat	
	Independents: 3 seats	

Date	Breakdown of Seats	Prime Ministers
June 30, 1996	**"Democratic Union" Coalition** (Mongolian National Democratic Party, Mongolian Social Democratic Party, Mongolian Worshipers Democratic Party, and the Green Party): **50 seats** MPRP: 25 seats Mongolian Traditional United Party: 1 seat	Mendsaikhany Enkhsaikhan (7/19/1996-4/23/1998) Tsakhiagiin Elbegdorj (4/23/1998-12/9/1998) Janlavyn Narantstasralt (12/9/1998-7/22/1999) Rinchinnyamyn Amarjargal (7/30/1999-7/26/2000)
July 2, 2000	**MPRP: 72 seats** National Democratic Party (MNDP): 1 seat Civil Courage Party: 1 seat Mongolian New Social Democratic Party: 1 seat Independent: 1 seat	Nambaryn Enkhbayar (7/26/2000-8/20/2004)
June 27, 2004	**MPRP: 37 seats** Motherland-Democracy Coalition (Democratic Party, Motherland Party, National New Party, Civil Will Party): 35 seats Republican Party (MRP): 1 seat Independents: 3 seats	Tsakhiagiin Elbegdorj (8/20/2004-1/25/2006) Miyeegombyn Ekhbold (1/25/2006-11/22/2007) Sanjaagiin Bayar (11/22/2007-9/11/2008)
June 29, 2008	**MPRP: 45 seats** Democratic Party: 28 seats Civil Will Party (CWP): 1 seat Green Party: 1 seat Independent: 1 seat	Sanjaagin Bayar (9/11/2008-10/29/2009) Sukhbaatar Batbold (10/29/2009 to 8/9/2012)
June 28, 2012	**Democratic Party: 33 seats** Mongolian People's Party: 25 seats **Justice Coalition (Mongolian People's Revolutionary Party and Mongolian National Democratic Party): 11 seats** **Civil Will – Green Party: 2 seats** Independents: 3 seats	Norovyn Altankhuyag (8/9/2012 to present)

Source: Breakdown of seats 1992-2008 from Inter-Parliamentary Union, http://www.ipu.org/parline-e/reports/ 2219_arc.htm; breakdown of seats in 2012 from the website of the State Great Hural (Parliament) of Mongolia, http://www.parliament.mn/en/state-great-hural/categories/2604/pages/4991; prime ministers from Alan J.K. Sanders, *Historical Dictionary of Mongolia*, 3rd ed. (The Scarecrow Press, Inc., 2010), pp. 587-588.

Author Contact Information

Susan V. Lawrence
Specialist in Asian Affairs
slawrence@crs.loc.gov, 7-2577